Grimoire
~ of ~
Magick

XZAVIER

Copyright © 2015 by Xzavier
All Rights Reserved.
ISBN: 1507608012
ISBN-13: 978-1507608012

Grimoire of Magick
Get the Android App Available on Google Play!

White Magick

HEALING SPELLS

Simple Healing Spell

You Need:
Rosemary Incense
Cinnamon Oil
Blue Candle

During each of the 4 main moon phases: New, Waxing, Full, Waning

Take Ritual Bath with pinch of rosemary .
Write the name of person in need of healing on blue candle. Anoint it with Cinnamon oil. Visualize healing energies flowing into candle. Burn candle for 4 minutes a day.

While visualizing, say:
"In the name of the goddess and god who breathes life into us all, I consecrate and charge this candle as a magical tool for healing."

Place the candle on top of a picture of the person in need of healing. Light the candle. As the candle burns, visualize the person in your mind, willing them the healing energies needed.

Chant these words four times:

Magic mend while the candle burns,
Sickness will end and health will return,
Harm to none, So Mote It Be!

When finished with the entire spell, dispose of stubs/ash in running water.

Heal Physical Pain

You Need:
Amethyst Crystal

Sit in a quiet place and clear your mind of everything you can. Take the amethyst and hold it in the hand that is closest to the hurt. If the pain is in the center of the body hold it in your writing hand. Imagine a soothing light collecting at your feet and draw it up slowly towards your head filling every part of the body. Whilst doing this say silently the following verse:

*"Bright light, shining light
heal my pain with all thy might."*

Repeat this as you move the light up through the body. When you reach the top of your head expand to fill outside the head with light for about a foot. Then return to where the pain is most concentrated, push all your healing energy into this area.

If this doesn't work the first time then repeat. You should feel better soon.

To end the spell repeat the verse again but finish with:
"So Mote It Be"

Healing Bath

You Need:
Silver or white candle
Salt
Healing oil (such as carnation, violet, sandalwood, or narcissus)

Take a lit candle, some salt, and your healing oil into the bathroom. By the candle's light run a tub of very warm water. Cast some salt into it, add a few drops of healing oil, and then step into the tub.

Relax. Feel the warm salted water sinking into your pores, through your skin, sterilizing the sick portions of your body. Visualize the pain/sickness leaving your body and leaching into the water. Then pull the drain plug and empty the tub.

While it is draining, chant:

The sickness is flowing out of me, Into the water, down to the sea.

Only when the tub is completely drained stand up. It is best to immediately splash your body with fresh water (a shower is ideal) to remove the last vestiges of the disease of sickness-laden water. Repeat as needed to speed your body's recovery.

<u>Healing Energy</u>

Use healing energy with physical pain or sickness; can also be used for spiritual pain or emotional pain.

Put your dominant hand out with your palm facing up.

Move energy from your heart to your palm, and visualize the energy a light blue color forming in the palm of your hand.

Don't put too much thought into it, just feel it.

Once you feel the energy stirring through your palm, place in on the part of your body that hurts.

If it's a sickness, place it on your forehead.

If it's emotional, place it on your heart.

If it's spiritual, place it on your throat.

When you do this you should feel a warm sensation.

If you do not feel the warm sensation, don't give up, try again.

<u>Banishing Grief</u>

You Need:
1 Smokey Quartz Gemstone
1 Bowl of water
3 table spoons of sea salt

Hold the quartz in your power hand. Visualize the grief transferring from you, to your hand, into the quartz. While doing so say,

*"Banishing stone,
Fill yourself with my grief,
So that I may feel joy again,
So mote it be!"*

Stir the mixture of sea salt in the bowl of water counterclockwise then add the smokey quartz.

Swish the stone around three times in a counterclockwise motion.

Leave the stone in the water for a few minutes, then take the stone outside and safely throw it as far as you can away from yourself.

Crystal Healing

You Need:
A Crystal
Fresh Spring Water
Sea Salt

First purify the crystal by washing it in salt water then rinsing it in pure spring water.

Hold it in both hands, close your eyes.

Imagine yourself with the healing energy of the crystal.

The same time, imagine yourself bathed in a stream of pure energy which runs from the crystal through your hands and into your body.

When you have done this make sure you sleep with the crystal under your pillow at night or on a bed stand near your head.

<u>Fever Healing Spell</u>

You Need:

Piece of paper
Pen or Pencil
A Piece of String

Write the following on a piece of paper and wrap it around the fevered persons neck with the string:

ABRACADABRA
ABRACADABR
ABRACADAB
ABRACADA
ABRACAD
ABRACA
ABRAC
ABRA
ABR
AB
A

Once placed around the persons neck,
the fever will vanish just as the words do.

Healing Potion

You Need:
Equal Parts;
Rose Mary leaves
Peppermint leaves

Put them in a pot of boiling water and wait until it has the look tea might have. Then put in a spray bottle and spray it on wound.

Healing Powder

You Need:
2 parts Eucalyptus
1 part Thyme
1 part Myrrh
1 part Allspice

Mix together and sprinkle on the bedding or in the room of someone under the weather to help speed up the healing process. Can also be scattered on your altar and under a blue candle when doing a healing ritual.

Notes on using Powders:
Be sure to finely grind up the herbs used in the powders.

Starting in the East, sprinkle the powder around you in a clockwise motion and then sit within the circle to absorb the energy from the powder.
Sprinkle the powder around a candle before burning to increase the candles energy.
You can sprinkle the powder on your altar before spell-work. Use the appropriate powder for the ritual.

Cure Sickness

You Need:
8 inch length of cord/string/rope/yarn
(whatever you have on hand)
Pen and paper
Container of salt

Mark the cord six times so that you have -seven- equal lengths. Take a few deep breaths and feel your energy connecting with the earth. Repeat the following words six times while you tie a knot in the cord each time:

"Sickness, no one bids you stay,
Its time for you to fade away,
Through these knots I bid you leave,
By these words which I do weave."

Put the cord in the container of salt. Create a seal for the container with the above incantation written on the paper. Dispose of the container, in running water if possible.

The number six has particular relevance here: it is widely accepted as the number of the Sun, which is restorative and regenerative.

HEX BREAKING SPELLS

Hex Breaker

You Need:
1 sprig of rosemary
1 piece of yellow paper
1 red pen
1 red cloth
Paprika or red pepper
1 piece of red cotton

While you are performing the spell, carry some rosemary at all times. Write the person's name on the piece of yellow paper. If you're not sure of the name of the person who's placing the curse on you, just write down the words 'enemy of mine.'

Using the red pen, draw a figure of a doll shape around the name and then cut out the shape with your scissors. Lay the paper doll face down on the red cloth and sprinkle it with the paprika. Tie the red cotton around the middle of the paper doll and then wrap it up in the red cloth. Hold the wrapped doll in your hand tightly and repeat these words:

"Enemy mine your power is gone,
The hex is broken The spell undone,
The eye has been turned away,
Enemy mine you've gone away,
So shall it be from this day."

Perform this spell for seven consecutive nights at midnight. On the next Sunday, unwrap the paper doll and tear it into nine pieces, then burn it. Scatter the ashes far from your home and throw the remaining red cloth into the garbage.

Reverse A Curse

You Need:
3 white candles
A mirror
Organic soap
Sea salt

Set the three white candles decoratively around a mirror, one you can be seated across from in a meditative pose.

Light the candles.

Assume a meditative stance. Cross your legs, straighten your back and relax your shoulders. Place your hands on your knees with your palms facing up. Raise your chin and face directly into the mirror.

Begin deep breathing. Inhale through your nose and hold the air in your lungs for five seconds. Exhale through your nose and keep your lungs empty for another five seconds.

When your mind is clear of all mental static, visualize your target. Imagine the curse seeping out of you through your pores in the form of a vile liquid. Imagine the liquid seeping up from the floor, to the wall, to the mirror, where the caster of the curse's reflection has replaced your own. Imagine their image being saturated in the vile liquid beyond any recognition.

(Continued next page...)

Recite the following incantation:

With this spell may I reverse,
This miserable word of curse.
Let all the misery it hath wrought,
Be brought to they, and they to naught.
Let not this simple spell coerce,
Or make my situation worse.
Hear now my humble plea,
As I will it, so mote it be.

Draw a warm bath or shower. If bathing, sprinkle salt into the water in a clockwise rotation. If showering, sprinkle salt around the basin of the shower in a clockwise rotation. Then, bathe thoroughly with organic soap.

When you wake up the next morning, the curse will be lifted.

Banishing Spell

You Need:
4 small pieces of paper
Something to write with
A black candle
A toothpick or something to carve the candle
Matches or a lighter

Get four small pieces of paper and on each piece write the persons name or the name of whatever it is you need to banish. On the opposite side draw a pentacle. Write the same name on the pentacle and carve it on the black candle.

Do what you would normally do as far as visualizing this thing or person being drawn away from you. At this time ask any deities or personal patrons for help if you'd like. Light the candle. Take the four pieces of paper and burn one, saying, *"I banish *NAME* with the power of fire. So mote it be."*

Bury one in some dirt, saying,
*"I banish *NAME* with the power of Earth. So mote it be."*

Flush one down the toilet, saying,
*"I banish *NAME* with the power of Water. So mote it be."*

Then tear one into little pieces and throw it out your window, saying, *"I banish *NAME* with the power of Wind. So mote it be."*

Let your black candle burn down.

If you prefer to work outside, you can obviously use a stream instead of your toilet.

Banishing Evil Spirit

You Need:
Bay leaves
Cinnamon
Rose petals
Myrrh
7 White candles
Paper and pencil

Crush equal parts of the herbs and make into an incense to burn during spell. Light the candles then cast a circle.

Invite deities and or elements you want to help you (optional)

Either draw a pentagram on paper or in the air with your wand for protection.

Visualize what you think the spirit looks like, then imagine a ball of white light forming inside of it and expanding until it makes the spirit explode.

Say:
"Begone evil spirit,
Begone from my life,
Begone from my house,
I want no strife,
Return to your master,
And bring them the word,
That I am untouchable,
Just like a swift, flying bird.

Imagine the spirit leaving you and going back to where it came from and exploding again.

Binding Harmful Person

You Need:
Paper
Black pen
White candle
Salt
Circle mirror
Black thread/cord/string anything really
Basil sage and angelica incense

Cast a circle
Light candles and incense
Write down the persons name on a small piece of paper with the black pen.

Start wrapping the paper in the black cord saying:
"(name of person) I bind you from bringing harm"

Repeat until paper is completely wrapped.

When done light the paper from the flame of the candle and imagine their power to harm burning away.

When burned down place the remains on the mirror and make a small circle of salt round the ashes.

Concentrate on the person and then breathe on to the mirror and say *"evils death by my breath."*

Close the mirror and seal it with the black candle wax then bury until the person has stopped there negative behavior.

Return A Hex

You Need:
3 black candles

If you are certain that someone has hexed you, return it to them using the following spell; but use it wisely - if you're wrong about the hex the spell can backfire.

This must be done for three nights in a row during a waning moon just after sunset.

Light three black candles, and as they burn, say the following verse:

Broken this spell, broken this curse,
By these candles, by this verse,
Reflected back, three times three,
Your hexes have no effect on me,
Curse return, by candles three,
Burn away and set me free,
Live and learn, crash and burn,
Three times three, this hex return,
With harm to none, this lesson be told,
Whatever is sent out, returns three-fold.

On the third day allow the candles to burn themselves out.

Curse Breaker

You Need:
1 Black candle
Water
1 Black bowl
1 Lighter or set of Matches
1 Shovel

Light the candle, place it into the black bowl. Fix the candle to the bowl using the wax dripping from the candle so that it stands alone.

Fill the bowl to the rim with fresh water and without wetting the wick.

Breathe deeply and meditate for a couple of minutes. Visualize the power of the spell cast against you as living within the candles flame.

As the candle burns down, it will sputter and go out as it touches the water.

As it is extinguished by the water, the spell is broken.

Dig a hole into the ground, pour the water into it and then bury the candle.

Anti-Curse Burn Ritual

You Need:
1 tablespoon sandalwood powder
1 tablespoon frankincense
1 tablespoon myrrh
1 cup pine needles
Charcoal - to burn ingredients after mixing them

Grind the above ingredients into a potent powder. Then, chant the following incantation three times in the silence of the night:

"Goddess of Light, I ask of thee to remove that which binds me.
With the power of the night, your aid I seek thee.
Dark moon's light, free me, deliver me.
So mote it be."

Focusing your energies and that of the night sky, transfer the negative energies of the hex into the ingredients. Then, take a bath, channeling your own energies to take the place of the hexes' force.

After the bath, meditate to drive any remaining curses/hex energy from one's system and chakra flow into the ingredients. Then, burn the ingredients until nothing but powder is left. With the ingredients burned, so is the curse defeated and out of one's system.

Anti-Hex Charm Spell

You Need:
A Small Apple Twig
A Hair From Your Head

Wrap the hair around the twig while saying:

*"Whoever it is that hexes me,
Could hex themselves by the power of three.
As I wish them no harm, I'll bind their power,
To the safety of a tree this hour"*

Place the twig and hair in the branches of a nearby tree.

Evil Eye Removal

You Need:
Black cumin seeds
Paper/paper bag
Fire

Wrap an odd number of black cumin seeds in paper or place them in a paper bag.

Pass this packet around the victim of the evil eye three times

Burn the paper bag in the fire.

When you hear the seeds snap, crackle and pop you'll know the evil eye has cracked up also. If no sounds are heard further action needs to be taken, by repeating the process.

LOVE SPELLS

Simple Love Spell

Write on a piece of paper:

"Goddess of love,
Please grant me my wish
to win (name)'s love
so we can live happily ever after.
I will dream of him,
He/she will dream of me,
SO MOTE IT BE"

"So mote it be" must be written as big as possible. Fold it in half and spray perfume on the paper. Draw a heart on the on one side of the paper and a pentagram on the other side. Now every time you go to bed, hold the paper and say:

"Goddess of love,
Please grant me my wish
to win (name)'s love
so we can live happily ever after.
I will dream of him,
He/she will dream of me,
SO MOTE IT BE"

After that, kiss the piece of paper and hide it under your pillow or in your pillowcase. Repeat this every night before bed until your love comes to you!

Find A New Love

On the night of a New Moon, cut a red heart out of paper.
On the heart write:

*"As this heart shines in candlelight,
I draw you to me tonight"*

Light a single white candle.
Hold the heart in front of the flame and let the candlelight shine on it. Then read what you wrote out loud 3 times.
Place the heart and spell in an envelope.
Seal it with wax from the candle. Conceal the envelope and leave it untouched for one cycle of the Moon (28 days).
By the time the Moon is New again, there should be new love in your life.

Bring Back Lost Love

Light the following candles:

A red candle (South)
A green candle (North)
A yellow candle (East)
A blue candle (West)
Two pink candles

Position the candles at the corresponding corners. Hold the two pink candles in your hands and face the red candle (south).

Chant the following until you feel satisfied:
"Beautiful Goddess, powerful God, hear my prayer! Lords of fire, burn my desire, times three If it is meant to be, Bring *NAME* back to me."

Attract Love Powder

You Need:
1/4 cup corn starch
2 teaspoon cinnamon
1 teaspoon ginger
1/2 teaspoon ground cloves

During a Friday night, Mix the ingredients together, while thinking of love coming into your life and feeling happy.

Keep the perfume powder in a container and dust yourself with it after taking a shower or bath.

Love Knot Spell

You Need:
1 Pink piece of yarn (pink~love)
1 Red piece of yarn (red~passion)
1 White piece of yarn (white~purity)

Tie a knot near one end of the braid as you visualize a new love arriving in your life.

As you tie the knot, say the following chant:

"Venus, Queen of Love, divine
Bring the love to me that's mine."

Braid the three strings together as you continue to visualize the perfect romantic partner falling deeply in love with you as you fall in love with him/her. Really try to feel the emotions of the two of you being happy together, being romantic, kissing and smiling, etc.

Next tie another knot and repeat the chant as you continue the visualization. Do this a total of seven times (knot and chant, braid and visualize, knot and chant), until you have seven knots in the cord. Keep the knotted string with you (you may wish to fashion it into a necklace or bracelet and wear it) until you find your perfect love. After you have found love, keep the cord in a safe place. If you decide you want to end the relationship someday, you can use the cord in a ritual designed for that purpose.

<u>Love Song Spell</u>

You Need:
Bowl of water
Sea salt
A song that reminds you of your "love"
1 pink candle
7 Red rose petals

In the bowl of water add three pinches of salt.

Light the pink candle and place it in front of the bowl.

Hold the rose petals in your hands then play the song and chant:

This song, sweet music flows from your heart to mine,
Our love will last till the end of time,
With this sound you will come to me,
And bind our love, So Mote It Be!

Repeat this until the song is over then blow out the candle.

Place the rose petals in the bowl of water then place the bowl in a place where it will not be disturbed.

Leave it until all the water has evaporated.
At this time the spell is complete.

Create A Crush On You

You Need:
Red string or yarn approx. 7 inches long
Focus your intentions, and fixate their face within your mind.
Try to tie each knot at least an inch apart. Now say:

"With Knot of one, this spells begun" {Tie the FIRST knot}

"With Knot of two, I call to you" {Tie the SECOND knot}

"With Knot of three, you will come to me" {Tie the THIRD knot}

"With Knot of four, your heart wants more" {Tie the FOURTH knot}
"With Knot of five, your passion is alive" {Tie the FIFTH knot}

"With Knot of six, your desires are fixed" {Tie the SIXTH knot}

"With Knot of seven, being mine is your heaven" {Tie the SEVENTH knot}
"With Knot of eight, a crush I create" {Tie the EIGHTH knot}

"With Knot of nine, your heart is mine" {Tie the NINTH knot}

Loop the yarn or cord around to form a circle and knot it.

Now say:
"With this last knot, making ten,
Your crush on me, now begins!
SO MOTE IT BE!"

Make sure you have the knotted cord with you at all times!

Attract Love Bath

You Need:
Clove
Daffodil
Rose
Vanilla
Salt
Plastic bag

Pour 3 daffodil petals, 3 rose petals, about two drops of vanilla, a teaspoon of clove, and about half a cup of salt into the plastic bag.

Shake it up then when ready pour the newly made bath salts into a warm bath.

Chant 3 times:

"Dear goddess Isis please let love come to me, with your power let it be."

__Make Someone Think Of You__

You Need:
1 mirror
picture of him or her
picture of you

Take the mirror and on the side where you see your reflection place his/her picture facing the mirror, on the other side facing inward place your picture and tape both securely, on the back of your picture write these words and hold the mirror close to your heart and chant 3 times:

"With these magic words I plea
Each time you see your reflection you will think of me
This is my will, so mote it be!"

Keep the mirror in your purse or pocket but carry it with you wherever you go for 30 days you will see the results long before this but it could take up to 30 days.

<u>Desire Me Oil</u>

You Need:
3 drops of lavender
Orange blossom oil
1 drop of lemon oil
Red Candle
Pink Candle

Mix the oils together to make the "Desire Me Oil"

Speak the name of your desired and bless your work. Every day, light the candles and anoint them with Desire Oil and let them burn for 2 hours.

Meditate on your beloved being with you for at least 15 minutes (and up to 2 hours) each day while the candles burn.

Then snuff the candles out - DO NOT BLOW THEM OUT!!!

Repeat daily until your beloved responds to you.

When you will be near your beloved, dab a tiny bit of the Desire Oil on your forehead and in the middle of your chest.

PROTECTION SPELLS

Protection Spell

You Need:
Staff or wand - blue or silver (you can use a ribbon or cloth to cover your wand then remove it later)
Silver or blue shiny glitter
A quiet place - best done outdoors

It is best to go outside for this spell as the air movement will help disperse the glitter and the magick. Cast a circle or create a sacred space.
Go to each quarter in turn (starting at west, then north, east, south) and pound or tap on the ground with the staff or wand chanting :

"I call thee, who guard the watchtowers of the (insert direction here) to guide me through the darkness, and ensure my safety."

Do this for all 4 quarters.

Stand in the center and Chant:
"In the shadows, evils hide,
Ready to draw me from love's side,
but with your help I shall be strong,
Banish all that do me wrong,
Send them away, send them astray,
Never again to pass my way.
So mote it be!"

As you say the last three lines, scatter the glitter in a circle around you. Close the circle and have something to eat to restore your energy.

Protect Your Home

You Need:
Salt
Cups
Any object of value to you
Bowl
Clean Water

Before you start, keep the object of value close to you. It resembles bravery, strength, and determination.

Take the cups and pour salt into each of them so you can't see the bottom of the cup

Place the cups in every room. For large rooms, you should probably have 2.

If there's already something that can harm you in your home, place the cups by entrances. If it's a strong force, you should pour some salt into bowls and place them around your home.

Sit down in a relaxed place.

Pour clean water into the bowl

Keep your hands in the water for 30seconds. This will clean your hands in case anything might have unknowingly harmed you.

Ghost Powder

You Need:
1 part dried rosemary leaves; ground
1 part sea salt
1 part garlic powder

Blend the ingredients and seal the powder a glass container.

If there is a ghost or spirit in your home, try to observe its behavior. Note in which room it is most often seen, felt, or heard, and pay special attention to its coming and goings.

Sprinkle the Ghost Powder so as to make a barrier across the place where it enters your space.

Also sprinkle the powder where it exits, but be sure to do this when it is not present, so that you do not trap it in your home!

Evil Trap Bottle

You Need:
Garlic
Needles
Pins
White Vinegar
Glass jar with metal lid
White candle

Gather together rosemary, needles, pins and red wine. Fill the jar with the first three, saying while you work:

"Pins and needles, garlic and vine, evil is trapped in this bottle of mine."

While you are filling the jar, visualize the evil energy being sucked into the jar.

When the jar is as full as you can get it, pour in the vinegar. Then cap or cork the jar and drip wax from the candle to seal. Bury it at the farthest corner of your property or put it in an inconspicuous place in your house.

The bottle destroys negativity and evil, the pins and needles impale evil, the vinegar drowns and dissolves it, and the garlic purifies and sends it away. It works unobtrusively like a little powerhouse and no one need know that it is there.

Dream Protection

You Need:
1 tablespoon lemon juice
1 tablespoon sea salt
1 table spoon vegetable oil
1 light weight cauldron or a glass bowl
1 piece of paper
Black pen
2 black or red candles (one of each works best)

Mix the lemon juice, sea salt and oil into the cauldron or bowl. Place the cauldron in front of you on the floor. Sit comfortably and place the candles beside the cauldron, red on left, black on right. Rip the paper in half then set it aside. Light both candles, left one first.

Now close your eyes and visualize a sphere. See the black and red candles burning around you.
Watch as the candles spin around you, getting faster each time they pass. Then see yourself magickally being released.
On one piece of paper draw a picture of what you saw. On the other, write down your biggest fear.

Light both pieces of paper on fire using black candle for the written half, red candle for the drawing

Then throw them into your cauldron. After the flame goes out, take the cauldron outside and pour everything in it into a hole in the ground. Then cover the hole with dirt, the spell is now complete.

Protective Circle

You Need:
Something to draw with (salt or chalk work best).
Something to draw it on.
A protective circle design.
4 Rail road spikes.
Brick dust.

Lay down your circle, put railroad spikes down in the 4 directions with the point out, and chant:

"As this circle down,
None evil here maybe found,
I am protected within,
Enemies can't get me, they can't win,
I step into this hallowed place,
darkness be gone and light give chase."

Step inside your circle.

Lay down the brick dust, no enemy can cross it if they mean you harm.

Witches Cleansing Jar

You Need:
Sand
Glass jar (like a big pickle or jam jar)
Rosemary
Lemon peel
Sage
Cedar
Black peppercorns
Lavender
Dill
Bay leaf
Rowan
Candle for wax seal
Permanent marker

To make an witches cleansing jar, pour a layer of clean sand into the jar. Add layers of dried herbs, one at a time.

When the bottle is full, focus cleansing protective energy into the herbs and sand, and see a golden light radiating from the bottle.

Visualize the herbs driving away negative influences. Cork and seal the bottle with white wax. Using a permanent marker, draw a pentagram (point facing up) on one side of the bottle, and on the other side draw an inverted pentagram (point facing down).

Set the bottle near your front or back door, and every six months, uncap, pour herbs out into the woods, garden, or your compost heap, and thoroughly wash and dry the bottle before filling it with a new round of herbs.

Protection Potion

You Need:
1/2 Cup of Spring Water
1 Teaspoon Vervain
2 Tablespoons Sea Salt
2 Tablespoons each of Frankincense and Myrrh
Jar for mixing

Mix all ingredients in a jar or whatever you have handy.

Sprinkle potion very lightly around home in discreet places (i.e., in closets) and anoint the bottom of your shoes and those of loved ones.

Dispose of remainder immediately after use.

Protect and Purify A Room

You Need:
4 pennies made in the year of your birth
5 candles to represent the elements

Put one penny in each of the four corners of the room.

Cast a circle with the five candles as you normally would.

Face each candle (starting with north) and repeat the following for each one:

*"Pennies from heaven, pennies from earth,
Marked with the magickal year of my birth,
Protect this room and all inside,
Safe and pure no need to hide"*

When you get to the final candle and complete the incantation, the room should now be cleansed of all negativity, and can now be used as a protective shell of sorts for whoever often occupies the room for as long as the pennies remain.

Protective Necklace Charm

You Need:
A necklace, any one you wish to charge

Take the necklace and hold it in your power hand (the hand that you write with.) Visualize a bright warm light around it. Now imagine a force field around you warding off evil.

Say: *"I call upon the universe, to make this my protective charm. When ever I wear it, I shall endure no harm."*

Imagine the light soaking into the necklace, and then you're done!

GRAY MAGICK

LUCK SPELLS

Good Luck Jar

You Need:

Buckthorn Bark	Mistletoe
Chamomile	Mojo Wish Bean
Clover	Myrrh
Dandelion	Nutmeg Peony Root
Frankincense	Queen of the Meadow
Heal-all	Rose Hips
Honeysuckle	Rosemary
Huckleberry Leaves	Sacred Bark
Irish Moss	Sandalwood
Job's Tears	Spearmint
High John the Conqueror	Star Anise
Khus-khus	Thyme
Lotus	Tonka Bean
Lucky Hand root	

Fill a jar with an even combination of the magickal herbs listed above.
Seal the jar tightly and keep it in your kitchen on a shelf or on a windowsill. Place your hands upon the jar each morning after you wake up and say:

"To God and Goddess do I pray
Guide me through another day
Let good fortune come my way
Good luck hither, now I say."

After citing the magickal incantation, gentle shake the jar a few times and then kiss it before putting it back.

Good Luck Candle Spell

You Need:
One 7 day candle
Dragons Blood Oil
Water
Saucer
Paper
Pen

Fill your saucer slightly with some water.

On the paper write the what area you would like your good luck in.

Fold up the paper and place on the saucer in the water.

Now anoint your candle with the dragons blood then put it on the paper and light it.

Each night before you sleep visualize your desires being obtained.

On the 7th day snuff out the candle and dispose of it away from your property.

A White candle is the default for this spell. This spell can be customized by using different colored candles.

(See the Candle Magick section of this book!)

Lucky Necklace

You Need:

A piece of yarn or string(enough to fit around your neck)

A trinket with a hole in it(enough for the yarn/string to go through)

A green candle

Light the candle and loop the string in through the trinket and tie it.

Place the trinket in front of the candle and chant:

*"I charge this item and power it up,
forever I'll have it, it means good luck!"*

Repeat this twice!

Then take a drop of the candle wax and anoint the trinket.

Repeat the chant once more.

Then wear the "necklace" around your neck.

Ring Of Fortune

You Need:

Holy water
Salt
Clover
Silver ring

To make this work you must set up a room with no sound and no other people but you if there is they will get the luck and all the luck in you.

Put the salt and the clover in a bowl and crush them together.

Now put the ring in the mixture.

Then chant 3 times;

*"Ring of silver,
ring of power,
bring me fortune,
every hour"*

The power of good fortune is now in the ring.

When ever you wear it you will have good luck!

<u>Good Luck Ribbon</u>

You Need:

Green candle
Green ribbon an inch thick 6 inches long
A black marker

Take the green candle and light it.

Next take the green ribbon and place it between you and the candle.

With the marker write your initials.

Then chant 6 times:

*"Grant me fortune and good luck,
with good luck may I be struck,
so mote it be!"*

Take the talisman ribbon and tie around your wrist
(having excess is okay just tie into a bow and leave some room).

You may take it off and put it back on as you wish.

Snuff out the candle.

Good Fortune Mantra

You Need:

4 White candles

Cast a circle.

Sit in the center and place a candle in each position; North, South, East, and West.

Chant the following 7 times:

*"Powerful magick bring to me,
in this life the luck I need,
so all my desires can be seen,
and thus fulfill my every dream,
combined with earth and fire,
bring forth my hearts desire,
guardians of the air and sea,
keep all evil from harming me."*

Snuff the candles out in reverse order you lit them.

Close the circle.

<u>String Of Luck</u>

You Need:

White cord/string/yarn approx. 12" long

Tie four knots in it spaced as evenly as possible, saying as you tie each knot:

One knot for luck,
Two knots for wealth,
Three knots for love,
Four knots for health.

Repeat until all the knots are tied.

Keep the knotted cord with you as much as possible.

Flames Of Fortune

You Need:
1 orange candle
1 magenta candle
1 black candle
1 Own color candle

Light the candle representing yourself (that with your own color) and say:

"This is me (name or magickal name), everything I am."

Light the black candle and say:

"This is my bad luck. Leave me now and never return, drain away as the candle burns."

Light the orange one and say:

"This one represents the changes of good, I welcome them as I should."

Light the magenta candle and say:

"This is astral energy that I need to change, fill me full, flow like rain."

Now sit and chant until the candles burn out:

"I welcome change, I welcome good, I enjoy my life, as I should."

The candles must be allow to burn completely...

Purple Luck Pouch

You Need:

1 Green Leaf [any]	A bowl
1 Yellow Flower [any]	A handful of dirt
1 Blue Flower [any]	1 purple drawstring bag

Hold the leaf in your power hand:

"This leaf I did pluck, it's now mine, please bring me luck."

With the leaf still in your power hand, pick up the yellow flower in the same hand:

"Yellow flower in Earth did grow, On me, please, good luck bestow."

Now the blue flower while still holding the leaf and yellow flower:

"Color of Spirit at your behest, I ask by this spell that I be blessed."

Place the three in the bowl, and as sprinkling the dirt over them, say:

"As I sprinkled with Mother's soil,
Must work hard and I must toil,
if I am to have my will,
make it good, no harm, no kill"

Focus on the bowl and repeat the last invocation twice more, seeing yourself gaining luck. Once you feel it is fully charged, pour the contents in the purple bag and place it somewhere where it will not be disturbed.

Lucky Charm Creator

You Need:

7 White candles
Any Object you wish to charge with good luck.

Line all 7 candles up in a row in front of you.

Make sure you are positioned in front of the middle candle.

So you should have one directly in front of you and 3 on your left and 3 on your right.

Place the object in front of the candle in the middle.

Start on your right side and say the following:

*"Candle burns, flame is bright,
make this my lucky charm tonight"*

Then snuff out the candle and repeat with the next one.

Do this for all the candles but save the middle one for last!

Keep the object with you as always.

MONEY SPELLS

Simple Money Spell

You Need:

A green candle
Coins
A saucer

Carve and dress a green candle to express your desires then place it on a saucer.

Arrange coins around the base of the candle then light the candle and chant:

*"Money grow, money flow,
candle burn, watch me earn,
money grow, money flow,
candle burn, watch me earn"*

Repeat 7 times then snuff out the candles.

Not only will this draw in money but now the coins you used are all charged with good luck.

Carry at least one in your wallet at all times for an extra kick!

__Quick Money Chant__

You Need:

A quiet place

Find a quiet place to relax where you will not be disturbed.

Sit and relax, breath nice and slow.

Visualize money coming towards you for several moments and then and chant:

"God and Goddess hear me say,
Please make money come my way,
Help me gain money every day,
Please listen and hear me as I say,
So mote it be!"

Cauldron Of Cash

You Need:

1 cauldron with water
1 green candle
7 coins

Most powerful during the full moon but you can do it whenever. Place the candle in the middle of the cauldron with water.

It's best for the cauldron to be in the view of the moonlight, so consider doing this one outside since it will help a lot.

Next up you light the candle. After lighting the candle speak these lines:

"Lucky Lady of the Moon,
Donate funds so ever soon,
Grant me favor,
Grant me gold,
Grant it now,
Before I'm old!"

After saying this drop a coin in the cauldron and repeat until all the coin are in. Allow the candle to burn until it reaches the water line and puts itself out.

If you can, leave your cauldron outside under the moon and stars over night.

Magick Money Jar

You Need:

7 pennies (or your version of a 1 cent coin)
7 nickles (or your version of a 5 cent coin)
7 quarters (or your version of a 25 cent coin)
Large Pinch of Ginger
Large Pinch of High John
Large Pinch of Basil
1 tall clean glass bottle or jar

Place all items into the bottle, put the lid on tight, shake and chant 7 times:

*"Copper glow and silver shine,
Amongst all others, make wealth mine."*

Leave the bottle where you leave your wallet/purse/change for 7 days then bury it as close as possible to the house.

Midnight Money Spell

You Need:
1 gold candle
6 green candles
9 white candles
Pine oil for anointing
Candles
Salt

All candles must be dressed with pine oil and then arranged as follows:

Gold candle in the center.

Green candles in a circle around gold candle.

White candles in a circle around green candles.

At one minute past midnight, trace a salt circle around the outermost circle of candles.

Light the gold candle first, then the green candles, moving clockwise, then the white candles, moving clockwise.

Circle the altar three times, chanting:

*"See the candles burning bright,
bring me money throughout the night,
Through the day and through tomorrow,
increase my wealth and end my sorrow."*

Do the chant 3 times. Sit quietly for a few minutes and visualize your monetary needs. Then snuff the candles in reverse order.

Money Moon Spell

You Need:
Glass of water
Silver coin

Put the coin at full moon best at midnight in a glass of water. Look that the reflection of the moons light is shined on the coin. Let the light of the moon reflect from the coin into your eyes.
Say 3 times: *"Lovely lady of the moon,*
Bring to me your wealth right soon,
Fill my pockets with silver and gold,
All as much my purse/wallet can hold."

Silver Coin Spell

You Need:

bowl	jasmine oil
one silver coin	2 gold candles
cloves (A pinch)	2 green candles
nutmeg (A Pinch)	

Light the candles and place either side of the bowl. Put the herbs in the bowl with the silver coin. Add 7 drops of jasmine oil and say the following:
"A silver coin starts my wish,
The money grows within this dish,
Every day the coins increase,
And never will they ever decrease."

Drip some wax over the herbs and coin. Then snuff out the candles. Add another coin to it each day. If you find any coins laying around, pick them up and add them to the bowl for extra effect.

More Money Charm

You Need:
A square of green cloth
Allspice
Borage
Lavender
Saffron
Crystals (such as garnet, ruby and emerald or rock salt)
Three silver coins
Gold and silver-colored thread

Hold the three silver coins in your hands.

Breathe on them four times and say:

"To the spirits of Air I say, bring some money my way."

Put the herbs, crystals and coins on the cloth.

Tie the cloth into a bag using eight knots in the thread. (It is probably easiest to fold the thread into two and tie knots round the neck of the bag.)

Hide the bag in a safe, cool, dark place, away from prying eyes for eight days.

After eight days money should be coming in. Be as realistic as possible, imagining what you will do with the money and how best it will be used.

Once you have made the bag, meditate daily on what you want. By using the three silver coins and four breaths you create the vibration of the number seven which is considered to be both a lucky, and spiritual, number.

Money Knot Spell

You Need:

Green 13-inch silk cord or ribbon

Chant this while tying knots in the cord/ribbon:

"By knot of one, my spell's begun."

"By knot of two, plenty fruitful work to do."

"By knot of three, money comes to me."

"By knot of four, opportunity knocks at my door."

"By knot of five, my business thrives."

"By knot of six, this spell is fixed."

"By knot of seven, success is given."

"By knot of eight, increase is great."

"By knot of nine, these things are mine."

Keep the knotted ribbon where ever you keep your wallet/purse.

Easy Money Spell

You Need:
1 Green Candle
1 Dollar Bill (or equivalent in your currency)
White String

Tie the string around the one dollar bill while saying:

*"Each time this string does turn,
my money grows, this I earn."*

After you finish tying the string, place the green candle on a small plate.

Place the dollar near the candle, but make sure no wax drips on the dollar.

I recommend putting the candle in the middle of the plate and placing the dollar on one of the edges of the plate. Light the candle and say:

"With each flicker of the flame, my money flows just like rain."

Now, let the candle burn until it's finished.

If the candle's flame goes out quickly, it means the spell took a shorter time to take effect.

SEX MAGICK

Simple Sex Spell

You Need:

Red Rose
Red candle
Vanilla incense

Take the red candle and set it on a flat surface.

Light the candle and say:

"Love and lust do not hide, bring my lover to my side."

Then place the vanilla incense by the candle and say:

"As the scent and smoke drifts by, my lover shall warm between their thighs."

Then spread the rose pedals and say:

"Red as rose I call to thee, to make him/her cum very hard for me, so mote it be!"

<u>Lust Spell</u>

You Need:

A red candle
A pen
Paper

Write your intended's name on the paper.

Light the candle.

Hold the paper above the candle with a corner touching while chanting the following:

"Let thoughts of (name) abound,

By this firelight, lust surround,

Their gentle smile and smolding gaze,

Make them alluring in all ways,

Make their spirit yearn for mine,

Hunger for me for all time,

Let their body crave just me,

By my words, so mote it be."

Lust Potion

You Need:

Patchouli oil
Sandalwood oil
Rose oil or Amber oil
Clove oil
Nutmeg oil
Olive oil

6 drops of Patchouli oil
6 drops of Sandalwood oil
6 drops of Clove oil
6 drops of Nutmeg oil
6 drops of Olive oil
And...
6 drops of Rose oil (For Attracting a male)
or
6 drops of Amber oil (For attracting a female)

Wear as a perfume whenever you'll be in the presence of the person you're trying to attract.

Recharge Libido Spell

You Need:
A tall red candle
Lavender oil
A quiet place

On a Monday night:

Before bed take a red candle and warm the wax by dipping it in boiling water. Carve 4 notches down the side equal distance apart.

Anoint the candle with the lavender oil into the candle and light.

Take off all your clothes.

Gaze into the flame and picture the most erotic thing you can think of. Just focus on the image in your head, picture every little detail so that you can almost feel it.

Touch the parts of your body you imagine your partner touching in your visualization.

DO NOT CLIMAX!

Keep the visual and touching going until the candle burns down to the first notch you carved.

Snuff the flame and go to bed.

Do this again the next night and the night after, by Friday night you will not only be ready for fun, but it will be amazing!

Sexual Desire Spell

You Need:

One red candle
Cardamon oil
Lavender incense

Light the incense and wait a few moments.

Take this time to relax and focus on your desired outcome.

Then, dress the red candle with the lavender oil and say the following:

"Fill my love with burning desire,
Burning for me like the hottest fire,
Let him/her think of me, feel me, want me much,
Let him/her desire my touch."

You must perform this spell for 7 straight nights.

Sexual Power

You Need:
1 Red candle
1 Pink candle
1 White candle

This is to be done right before you have sex.

Set the candles up in front of you. have your lover sit directly across from you.

White in middle.
Red on the (your)left.
Pink on the (your)right.

Speak the following words, you first, then your lover, then say it together:

"Spirits of the cosmos and all within, bring your shining stars to the flame,

Ignite the fires of our flesh, so that all our desires are kept fresh,

Spirits of the cosmos and all within, find favor in this spell,

Increase our passion and our love, let our lust burn as bright as the stars above,

Spirits of the cosmos and all within, bless our desires as we begin "

After you both have said this together - Begin making love and continue at least until the candles burn out!

Lustful Attraction

You Need:

100% Extra Virgin Olive Oil	* 1 Red
1 pinch Rosemary	* 1 Pink
1 pinch Cinnamon	* 1 Purple
1 pinch Lavender Oil	* 1 White
1 pinch High John	5 white Tea light Candles
4 Rocks (you can paint them the following colors)	2 Red Candles
	Small Bottle

Mix all of the herbs in a small bowl then place them in the small bottle with the olive oil and lavender oil and shake well. In a dark room set the rocks in a small circle, Facing the compass points. make sure the circle is no more than 1 foot across.

Place the Red Candles right outside the circle at the East and South points. Place the White candles inside the circle and form a Pentagram. Put the bottle in the center of the Pentagram. Light the candles and begin.

Recite:
"In this night,and in this hour,
I call upon the Ancient Power,
I draw out the feelings you hide so well,
These feelings you keep a secret, to me you will tell."

While you say the spell think about the person you are using it on. Visualize their feeling being drawn out and them acting upon those feelings. Then seal the top of the bottle and bury it with the rocks. This spell will draw out feelings of lust your intended has for you.

Orgasm Power

You Need:
Pen
Paper
A quiet place

This ritual is simply just using your sexual energy for your desired goal. Take your clothes off. Write down whatever you want your goal to be on the paper. Concentrate on your end goal. Stare at the words on the paper for a few minutes.

Now masturbate. If the end goal is the desire or love of someone that use that to masturbate to. If not, then just think of whatever gets your off.

DO NOT CLIMAX YET!!

Every time you get close to climaxing STOP! Bring yourself down a bit then build it back up - then STOP!!

DO this several times, you want to build the orgasm up as much as you can, then when you finally do climax: When you are right in the middle, picture that sexual energy firing from your body and accomplishing your goal.

Picture the outcome happening...see it happening as clear as you can. If you have not at this point got some of your fluids on the paper, make sure you anoint with it paper now.

Fold the paper 4 times and then throw it out.

This spell may have to be done more than once to get your desired result.

Passion Potion

You Need:

Some fresh lavender
A bottle of white wine
A red candle

Add the lavender to the white wine and allow to steep for 7 days.

Each one of the 7 nights, light the candle and say:

*"Who ever drinks this, will be mine,
in love and lust, my passion wine"*

After 7 nights its ready to go, simply strain and serve it and watch it work!

Dark Desire Smoke

You Need:

sweet grass	7 red candles
bay	lighter
sage	paper with subjects name on it
lavender	String or twine
salt	

Write the intendeds name on the paper, set aside. Draw a ring of salt. Light the candles around the circle, and sit inside it. Braid the bay, lavender, sage, and sweet grass together. you can use string to hold it together. Now burn it and let it smoke in front of you and say:

Chant:
"The darkest lust bound in this world, will burn ablaze passion unfurled, by these red candles power, by the magic that is born this hour!

I summon the lust that may reside, oh deep down flowing hot inside, my target who will now feel, the darkest passion, that will soon be real"

Inhale a little of the smoke.

Chant:
"By the night and by the day, by the moon and stars away, I summon all those spirits of lust, do my bidding because you must, now on this night and in this hour, I cast this spell with my power!"

Now burn the paper with the name on it.

SUCCESS SPELLS

Success In Court

You Need:
Several pieces of paper and a pen
Orange candle
Fireproof dish

Sit in a quiet space and light the candle. Breathe deeply several times to help clear your mind. Look at the issue from the perspectives of the other people involved (your opponents, the judge, jury and so on). Try to think of all possible scenarios which might occur, being realistic in your assessments. Write down each one on a single piece of paper.

See yourself handling each scenario calmly and factually. Concentrating on the candle flame, call on the gods and ask that there will be clarity, honesty and justice in the situation. Take a brief look at each of the scenarios again and write down any new ones which then come to mind. Now choose the outcome you most desire and put that piece of paper under the candle while it burns out. Take the rest of the papers and cut them up into small pieces. Set light to them in the fireproof dish by first lighting one piece from the candle. When these have burnt out, flush them away under the tap or blow them to the four winds. When you go to court, take the paper with your desired result, put it in your pocket, and when you find yourself in difficulties hold the paper unobtrusively in your hand to give you courage.

This spell does not automatically ensure that you will win your case, particularly if there is dishonesty involved. Remember that you are asking for justice, which may involve some kind of penance or penalty on your part.

Legal Success

You Need:

Your documents
High John Herbs
Deer's Tongue leaves
Calendula flowers
Cinnamon powder

Combine the leaves, flowers, herbs and ginger or cinnamon powder in equal measures.

Place your documents on a flat surface and sprinkle them thoroughly with the mixture.

Draw your finger nails through the mix in wavy lines from top to bottom. Concentrate as you do so on the desired outcome.

Leave the papers overnight then in the morning shake off the mix.

This spell does not seem to work if there is any dishonesty or deliberate nefarious dealings on your part.

However if you are completely in the right, it is possible to turn things in your favor.

Ritual Of Success

You Need:
Incense of your choice
Tarot card: Ace of Swords
A quiet place
A yellow votive candle
A needle
Matches

Sit comfortably on the floor or on a chair facing East.

Inscribe your initials onto the votive and place it to your left.

Place the incense to your right.

Place the tarot card directly in front of you.

Relax your body, spirit and mind.

Light the candle with the matches

Light the incense with the candle by picking up the incense and holding it over the flame.

Enter you meditative state and hold the card with both of your hands.

Meditate on the card while visualizing your self becoming successful and on what you would like to become successful in.

Do so for 10 to 15 minutes during a waxing moon
every day for a week.

Success In Business

You Need:

Three equal lengths of ribbon:
Dark blue for success in long-term plans, and clarity
Yellow for mental power, wealth, communication and travel
Orange for success and prosperity through creativity
A large safety pin

Pin the three ribbons together at the top to make braiding easier.

Braid the ribbons neatly together.

As you do so, repeat the following words as often as you feel is right remembering the significances of the colors:

*"Great Mother, Great Mother feel the energy flow,
As these strands become as one let my business grow."*

Now loop the braid around the front door handle so that anyone who comes into the business must pass it.

Find A Job Spell

You Need:
1 tsp ground cinnamon
1 tsp ground ginger
1 tsp ground lemon balm
Few drops of bergamot oil
Bowl

Mix all the ingredients together in the bowl.

For a dressing powder add a carrier such as powdered chalk or talcum powder which should be unscented.

To use as incense leave it as it is, and burn it on a charcoal disc in a heatproof burner.

Your papers (job application form) Any supporting documents (e.g. your CV/resume)

Light your incense. Before you begin writing or filling in your forms smoke the paper on which you will write. This consists of wafting the required amount of paper or the application form in the incense smoke and asking a blessing for the process you are about to start.

Once you have completed the forms or the writing you can dress each page individually. On the back of each page sprinkle the dressing powder

Draw your four fingers through the powder in wavy lines from top to bottom so they leave very clear tracks.

Leave for at least 1 hour, then shake off the powder, all the while visualizing the success of your project.

Dream Job Spell

You Need:
2 brown candles (to represent the job)
Green candle (for prosperity)
A candle to represent yourself
Prosperity incense such as cinnamon
Prosperity oil such as bergamot, or blended patchouli and basil

Light your prosperity incense. Anoint the candles with the prosperity oil from wick to end, since you want the good things to come towards you.

Place one of the brown candles in the center of your chosen space. Place the green one on the right, with your personal candle on the left.(These candles should be in a safe place; they have to burn out entirely.)

As you light your personal candle, say: *"Open the way, clear my sight. Bring me chance, that is my right."*

Light the green candle and say: *"Good luck is mine and true victory, Help me Great Ones, come to me."*

Light the brown candle and say: *"Openings, work, rewards I see, And as I will, So Must it Be."*

Leave the candles to burn out completely.
Each night for a week - or until the candle is used up - light the second brown candle for 9 minutes while contemplating the job and the good to come out of it. You need to identify exactly what you mean by a dream job. It is of little use aiming for something which is beyond your capabilities, though you might go for one initially which will begin to take you to where you want to be.

Artists Craftsmen Spell

You Need:
Red candle to represent energy and passion
Blue candle for wisdom
Smokey incense to represent the God's forge
The tools you use in your craft (paint brushes, pens, hammer, cloth etc.)

Place the red candle on the right of your sacred space, the blue on the left and your tools in between.

Put the incense in the middle above your tools.

Light your incense and build up a smokey atmosphere.

Light the candles, red first then blue.

Pick up the tool you use most, hold it up and say:

"Hephaestus, God of the forge,
Fashioned articles of beauty fit for the Gods,
Come to my aid,
Help me to create things of beauty as well."

Now pass your preferred tool through the smoke of the incense.

Hold it for a few moments, until you can feel its energy and sense it becoming alive in your hands, then say:
"Hephaestus I give you my thanks."

Inspiration Spell

You Need:

Cauldron
Seeds of wheat
High John herbs
Dragons Blood oil
White candle

Light your the candle.

Place the cauldron in front of you and half fill with wheat seeds, high john herbs and a splash of dragons blood.

Stir the cauldron clockwise three times and let the seeds trickle through your fingers as you say:

"Ceridwen, Ceridwen, I seek your favor for the power of Awen Inspiration to be what I must, grant me the gift of wisdom and poetic inspiration."

Since Awen is a threefold gift you should repeat the stirring of the cauldron twice more or alternatively once on each of the following two days. When you have finished bury the contents.

The candle may be snuffed out, but do not use it for anything else.

Pass Exam Spell

You Need:

Dried Sage
Dried Rosemary
Dried Thyme
Small purse or sachet

Take three small dishes of dried sage, rosemary and thyme, the herbs of memory and concentration.

Choose a book, a manual or notes you have made, to symbolize what you need to know or remember.

Scatter in turn a circle of each herb round the book, beginning with sage as the innermost circle, then rosemary and finally thyme, saying:

"Sage, rosemary, thyme, let this knowledge now be mine, In the circles three, memory increased be."

Gather the three circles of herbs into a small purse or sachet. Keep it with you while you study and place it under your pillow at night so you may learn while you sleep. You can also take it to an examination.

Mantra Of Success

You Need:

A moment to relax

Just take a few deep breathes relax and repeat:

*"I call upon the four Elements,
To guide me on the path to knowledge.*

*Keep my spirit off the edge,
Grant me Power,
Grant me Strength.*

*Grant me Wisdom,
I set my faith.*

*Earth, Fire, Water, Air,
Let me Succeed without Despair.*

So mote it be!"

BLACK MAGICK

ATTACK SPELLS

Soul Destroyer

You Need:
2 black candles
Dragon's blood incense
A personal possession (hair, clothing, jewelry, photo, etc.) from the victim
Black cloth
Black twine

Carve the name of your victim on one of the black candles. Then cast your magic circle. It should contain an inverted pentagram with the spirit point facing south.

Light the incense. Place the black candle without the victim's name on it on the fire point of your altar. Wrap your black cloth around the base of the black candle with the victim's name on it and light it. Use it to light the other candle. Then, place it across from you on the opposite side of the circle, with the name of your victim facing you.

Smooth the black cloth over the center of your pentagram. Pass the personal possession from your victim through the incense smoke, then place it on the black cloth.

Envision your victim. Imagine their soul being wrenched from their physical body through their crown and brow chakras. Visualize all the color draining from them and take pleasure in the thought of them being reduced to a soulless husk.

Chant the following:

*"From eternal fires
burning out of control
I open my jaws
and swallow your soul
This awful fate
you cannot foresee
As I will it, so mote it be"*

Fold the black cloth over the personal possession. Tie three knots in the black string from right to left, then tie it around the black cloth until it is bundled shut.

Close your magic circle.

Snuff out your candles in a counter-clockwise rotation.

Take the bundle and the remainder of the black candle with the victim's name on it in nature where it won't be discovered by cover of night. Light the remainder of the candle and place it somewhere close, being careful to avoid starting a fire.

Destroy the bundle, light it on fire or weigh it down with a stone and drop it in a lake. Whatever method of disposal you choose, pour the full force of your wrath into it.

Snuff out the candle and bury it.

Flame Of Death

You Need:

1 black candle
Wand
A personal possession of your target
An envelope

During a full moon, put the personal possession of your target into the envelope. Write his or her name on the front and back.

Place the candle on top of the envelope and light it.

Visualize the flame of the candle getting larger and hotter. Picture the fire growing into a large ball and flying off the candle and attacking your target.

Do this for several minutes until you can see it in your minds eye as if it is actually happening right then and there in front of you.

Then chant the following 13 times and keep picturing the fire ball getting stronger and flying towards your enemy:

*"Fire to fire, death to death,
mix them both with my next breath."*

On the 13th time, light the envelope and let it burn until its nothing but ashes.

Bury the ashes in dirt immediately.

<u>Death Doll</u>

You Need:

A branch from a lemon tree
A pentagram
A doll made of cloth (Cloth ONLY!)
Steel nails A picture of the target
5 black candles

Put the the pentagram on the floor / table. Place the candles at each point.

Pin the picture to the head of the doll. Now, place the doll in the middle of the the pentacle.

Light the candles in a clockwise rotation and say:

*"Pain upon you,
pain of death,
pain until,
your dying breath"*

Place a nail in the left hand of the doll. Then repeat the process in the following order:
Left hand
Right hand
Left leg
Right leg
Crotch
Head

Snuff out the candles then bury the doll with the nails in it outside and do not disturb.

Web Of Destruction

You Need:

Spider Webs
Charcoal
Parchment Paper
Black Cloth
Black Thread

Gather spider webs from your house.

Write on paper with the charcoal:

*"North South East West
Spider webs shall bind him best
East West North South
Breaks his limbs and shuts his mouth
Seal his eyes and choke his breath
Wrap him 'round with ropes of death!"*

Fold the paper 4 times then wrap with the spider webs.

Bind the cloth with the black thread wrapping exactly 9 times.

Then hang this in any dark corner undisturbed until it gets coated thickly with dust. Lastly, after this has happened, bury it.

Break Up A Couple

You Need:

Black candle
A needle

At midnight light the candle and take a pin and prick the candle many times over saying these words:

"As I prick this candle, I prick at thee,
Broken hearts unhappy be,
May you part soon one day,
Soon to go your separate ways"

Extinguish the candle. Take the candle and break it in half symbolizing and visualizing the splitting of the couple.

Then dispose of the two halves in separate trash containers once again visualizing them being completely apart from each other.

You may then go about your everyday events.

Cause A Divorce

You Need:
Clay
3 Black Cords
7 Black Candles
Scissors
Wand

Make two clay figures of a male and a female about 5" tall. So the two clay figurines represent the girl and the man itself.

Now bind the two figurines with three cords. (Necks, Waists, Feet)

Cast a circle and place the tied together figurines at the center. Around it, place candles in a circular pattern..

Now Visualize and concentrate on the candles. Visualize them as the hurdles that must be passed to get the divorce. After that take the scissors and chant this:

*"As I cut the first chord
let the bond be broken
never to be formed again
So mote it be."*

Cut the cord around the feet.

Repeat the chant and cut the cord from the waist. Then finally the one around the neck.

Snuff the candles out then dispose of the dolls in separate locations as far away from each other as you possible can.

Puppet Of Pain

You Need:
1 picture of the persons face
1 red puppet
A needle
Black thread
1 red candle
1 black candle
45 straight pins

Stitch the picture of the persons face into the head of the puppet.

Light the candles

Hold the pins one by one over the flames of both candles,

Stab the pins into different parts of the puppet, (Leg, arm, etc)

As you do, say the following each time:

*"Pain is hurt, hurt is pain,
feel my venom in your veins"*

Once all the pins are in the doll, set the doll on fire with the candle light and let it burn completely

Bury the ashes

Jar Of Despair

You Need:

Picture of the person you're wishing death upon
Salt
Oleander leaves
Jasmine berries
1 Large jar with lid
Hot glue gun
5 Black candles
Vinegar

Place the picture in the jar then add your poisonous plants.

Cast your circle then place the jar in the middle and say

*"Gods of death hear my cry,
cause my enemy to soon die,
with this jar, I do seal,
bring them death and make it real."*

Then pour the salt and vinegar in then seal the jar.

Once it is sealed pour the candle wax over it from each candle.

Then HIDE the jar in their yard.

<u>Slave Potion</u>

You Need:

Unscented body lotion
Geranium
Lemon juice
Sandalwood oil
Diluted rose oil

10ml unscented body lotion
2 drops lemon
1 drop geranium
1 drop sandalwood
20 drops rose oil

Blend well and massage into your hands.

Now if you shake somebody's hand they'll do anything for you.

Poisoned Ivy

You Need:

A piece of 3"x3" parchment paper
A leaf of poison ivy
A rubber band or piece of string
A pair of thick gloves (for protection)
A match or lighter

Write the person's name of which you plan to hex on the piece of paper.

Pick up the poison ivy (make sure you are wearing those gloves) and lay it on the paper over their name.

Careful to have the entire leaf of poison ivy on the paper roll up the paper.

Take the rubber band or string and bind the paper so it doesn't come unrolled.

Hold the paper over a lake or stream (anywhere with a good bit of water) and use the lighter or match to set the paper a flame.

Drop it immediately before you get burned into the water.

HEX SPELLS

Black Magick Curse

You Need:
Six unused black candles
Six nails
Six needles
Six pins / tacks
Two pieces of paper
Black pen / marker
Lighter / matches

Draw a six pointed star on one of the pieces of paper. It will turn out to look like David's star, but it's not.

Now take the candles and put one at each point of the star, and do the same with the nails, needles, and pins / tacks. Rip a small part of the second paper off and write the person's name you wish to curse on it. It's best if you have first, last, and (if they have one) their middle name written down, this way it will be more effective.

Light the candles in a counterclockwise motion. Make sure you know which candle you lit first, you will need to know this for the rest of the spell.

Take the paper with the person's name on it and burn a portion of it in the first candle you lit, then burn another portion in the second candle you lit, proceed to the third one you lit, and so on.

While doing this, say the following aloud, picturing them in your mind:

*"By Demons and Angels,
By Gods and Goddesses,
I curse _____,
As a punishment for all the hardships he / she has put me through.
This black curse,
This black power,
I curse thee."*

Only say the above chant once, otherwise it wont work.

By the time you get to the sixth and last candle, the whole paper should be burnt to ashes.

Blow out the candles in the REVERSE order in which you lit them, saying, "So mote it be!" when the FIRST candle you lit has been blown out.

Bones Of Anger

You Need:

Gather bones of chickens and dry them in the sun for a few days.
A bell

Then when you are ready to do this hex make sure you are worked up into a frenzy of anger and hatred. This will add to the potency of your hex! Be thinking of all this while doing this hex and when it says 'With these bones I now do crush" take a hammer or use your feet to stomp and crush these bones as if they were your enemy before you! When you are done sweep them up and place them in a bag. You will then want to sprinkle the dust and remains of the bones on your enemies property around his house.

Ring the bell 3 times and say...

"I call upon the Ancient Ones from the great abyss to do my bidding...

"Bones of anger, bones to dust
full of fury, revenge is just,
I scatter these bones, these bones of rage
take thine enemy, bring him pain
I see thine enemy before me now
I bind him, crush him, bring him down
With these bones I now do crush
Make thine enemy turn to dust
torment, fire, out of control
With this hex I curse your soul
So mote it be!"

Ancient Egyptian Curse

You Need:
Full moon
2 red and 2 black candle (tall)
Picture of those you wish to curse
Black sand

Go outside and place the candles around you then use the black sand to connect the candles and by doing that it should make a circle.

Now place the picture of the person you wish to curse in front of you and picture the worst thing to happen, then call upon Osiris, Anubis and Set to damn then to misery.

Once that is done let the gods take care of them.

Stone Hex

You Need:
Small stones - 1 for each letter in your enemies name.
Black marker
Cauldron
Water

Take a stone for each letter of your victims name and "baptize" it with its letter. Then toss it into the cauldron of water - there should be enough to cover the stones.

Heat the cauldron until the water inside begins to boil. Let stones boil until water is evaporated. After cooling throw the stones in a river or stream - MUST be running water.

Knots Of Chaos

You Need:
1 piece of thread or yarn about nine to ten inches long

You will tie 3 separate knots a couple inches apart as you recite the following...

"With this knot I seal this hex
you will not sleep, you will not rest
Knots of anger, knots of hate
Discord brings you to your fate.

I tie this second knot makes two
Bringing darkness over you
Slander, discord, evil too
Bringing darkness straight to you.

With this third knot, I do bind
Weaving chaos in your mind
Hex of anger, hex of hate
Bring him down, I will not wait"
So mote it be!

As you do this spell be thinking of all the chaos that it is going to bring to your enemy and make sure you are worked up into a rage before doing the spell. This will make it all the more effective!

When you are done see if you can hide this string (with the knots now tied) around you enemies home. This will make it more potent. If not then save it in a special place until you decide to untie the knots and give your enemy a second chance.

Enemy Moves

You Need:

Pen
White parchment paper
Picture of your enemy
Bottle of vinegar

When the moon is in a waning phase, write on white parchment paper the full name of the person you want to move, along with birth date if known.

Roll up the paper, with a photo if you have one, place inside a bottle of vinegar, then toss into a body of running water, visualize your enemy moving away as the bottle is washed away.

<u>Ugly Hex</u>

You Need:
Photograph of the person you are hexing
Bowl of water
Dirt

Direct your energies at the water and earth. Visualize them combining and being shapeable and moldable as mud. Imagine the water allowing the earth to be shaped and changed by your will. Now, release your energy into them to charge them while still thinking about this.

Combine the dirt and water, making mud. Taking the photograph of the person you seek to punish, spread the mud on the face. Visualize the changes to this person's appearance you wish to take place (teeth becoming crooked or discolored, becoming excessively fat, etc) and release energy into the photograph to lock the changes.

Finally, tear up the photograph and submerge the pieces in the bowl of mud. stir it until the pieces have become saturated and broken up within the bowl.

Now, just be patient. These changes will occur very slowly over time, and may keep going for many years.

Pain Doll Curse

You Need:

1 doll
Belonging of Who you wish to curse
3 Pins
1 Red Candle

At night, First light your candle then make sure your lights are turned off. Place the doll in front of you and the pins and the item of the person beside the doll. If the doll has buttons as eyes rip them off or cut them.

Then prick your finger with the pin and make yourself bleed. Only put one drop of blood on the belonging of the person you hate and one drop of blood on the doll. This will make them connected.

Once this is done the blood with seep into the doll, wait till it does do not force it. The say these words:

> *"This night it ends, I bring you pain,*
> *you're life will never be the same,*
> *I pierce the doll and start your fall,*
> *A slow decent, with pain and all."*

Then when you reach the end of it stab two pins in the dolls head and one when its heart is.

The next day something will be different about the person you hate so dearly.

Hex Vinegar

You Need:

Red wine	Camphor
Rosemary	Patchouli
Wormwood	
Rue	

Heat the mixture and boil for 13 minutes during a full moon. Strain and cap it tightly. Store in a cool, dark place.

Write your victims name on paper, and soak the paper in the vinegar. Allow it to dry and then burn it to be rid of your victim.

Lemon Rot Curse

You Need:

1 lemon	Picture of the intended
1 black candle	Black bowl
9 nails	Athame
Cursing oil	

Light the candle. Cut a slit in the lemon and place the picture of the person inside the lemon. As you visualize your anger toward the person, take one nail and pierce the lemon.

Take the remaining nails , one by one and pierce the lemon, until all the nails are in the lemon. Place the lemon in the bowl and cover it half way with the cursing oil

Place the bowl on your altar and let the lemon rot. As the lemon rots, so will the luck and life of the intended.

MISFORTUNE SPELLS

The Luxor Curse

You Need:

A pinch of black pepper
3 drops of lemon
Paper
Pen
A black candle

Write on the piece of paper these words:

"Luxor Nexor burst and burn,
Your luck now will surely turn,
From good to bad, from bad to worse,
You(the name of the victim) I now curse."

Then you put the pepper and the lemon drops on the paper and you fold it.

After that you light the candle and burn the paper.

The victim will experience extreme bad luck and great misfortune!

__Hellfire Curse__

You Need:
Three black candles
A bell

Light three candles at midnight Ring a the bell three times at the beginning of this ritual. Repeat the following incantation three times:

"I call to the mighty bringer of night,
Spirits of the abyss, here my call.
all most powerful one and all
Satan, my thoughts do sing
through the universe they now ring
Take thine enemy, make him smite
Break him, scorn him in the night
From the mighty depths of hell
Cast your darkness on his shell
Oh Satan, or shining star
Touch him, burn him from afar
Revenge now will have its day
for thine starts to fray
So mote it be!"

During the entire time in which this curse is being cast, be sure to concentrate yourself in the blood lust and fury and anger towards the person that this spell is cast towards. This spell will cause a person to be harassed demons. When you are done, extinguish the candles.

Blood Misfortune

You Need:

1 black candle
Chicken blood
Picture of your target
Red pen
Bowl

At midnight with a full moon:

Put the chickens blood in the bowl.

Write the name of the target on the picture.

Put the picture in the bowl.

Place the black candle in the bowl to hold down the picture.

Chant:
"Azazel, I call out to you to bring misfortune upon:
persons Full Name
Make him/her suffer until he/she goes insane,
No more happiness will be gained.
Pain, sickness, and hate they will find,
Forever and ever consumes their mind."

Blow out the candle. Go outside and dig a hole.

Pour the chickens blood and picture in the hole and cover it up.

The Dark Cloud

You Need:

Paper
Pen/pencil
Flame

Picture the person who you want cursed. Then Write his/hers full name on the paper, draw a dark cloud above the name and put the paper on fire. Then as it burns chant this:

"As your name shall burn
soon your luck will turn
with the power of the earth
you will soon regret your birth
with the power of the fire
your good luck will now expire
with the power of the water
you will be hated even by your mother
and with the power of the air
a dark cloud above your head you'll wear!"

When the paper is burned down say "*so shall it be*" 3 times.

Misfortune Chant

You Need:

A quiet place

Visualize dark energy around but not in yourself.

Now visualize this energy around the person you want to attack while visualizing a specific misfortune over and over.

Hold this visualization and affirm:
"(name the misfortune) is happening to (name)".

Affirm 5-10 times. Be sure to repeat this spell until the misfortune occurs.

Day Of Doom

You Need:
Paper
Pen

Write your targets name on the paper and fold it 5 times.

As you are folding it say:

"Misfortune all day, Misfortune all night. Bring bad luck to [person's name], till the next mornings light."

Carry the paper for the next 24 hours.

Gods Of Misfortune

You Need:

1 red candle
1 black candle
2 candle holders
Black string

Place candles in the candle holders. Place the black one on your left, the red on your right.

Tie the string to the candles so that the line is level in front of you.

"God of discord, ruler of chaos! I open the door to your domain!"
Now light the candles.

Visualize the string being the crossover point to the next dimension. Say the following:

*"Gods of chaos,
gods of discord,
obey me now,
for I'm your lord,*

*Attach your curse to -Targets Name-,
bring him/her misfortune for the rest of days,
afford them no relief of the devils gaze."*

Snuff the candles and keep the string tied tight.
To end the spell simply cut the string in the middle

Black Luck Hex

You Need:

Two black candles
Paper
Black pen
Black Chalk
Sage
Black Tourmaline

Purify area with sage.

Write victims name on paper and place in between black candles.
With the chalk, draw an upside down pentacle with upside down crosses on each corner, make sure it's around candles and paper.

Put the Black Tourmaline on the paper. Close your eyes and imagine the victims life being torn apart.

Chant 3 times:
"Your life in shambles, your life in dust,
your fortune gone, your luck and lust,
begone all that in which you are,
never regained, its gone to far."

Take the paper, and burn it. Leave the ashes where they are.

Close the circle.

Discord Spell

You Need:
1 black candle
1 piece of paper
1 long black thread
1 pen
lavender incense

While holding an image of your enemy in your mind write his/her name on a piece of paper then draw an inverted pentagram on it.

Fold it and then tie it to the black candle then as you light it chant:

"As this candle burns out so does order in your life, and as the candle burns out destruction shall enter your life."

Now chant this incantation 7 times (while visualizing your enemy getting what he/she deserves):

"Tenebrus potestas, Tenebrus potestas increscere timor et elicere morbus."

After you have recited the incantation visualize all that will happen to your target(make sure to include the limitations while visualizing) and how he/she must act towards you to break the spell.

Let the candle burn out or go out by itself once it does light some lavender incense to help it manifest, then carefully hide away the candle or its remains somewhere where it wont be disturbed and can only be found by you.

Talisman Of Doom

You Need:

1 piece of paper
Black chalk
A black pen
Matches

First draw a pentacle on the ground with the chalk.

Draw a circle around the pentacle with the chalk.

Take the pen and write the wrong doer's name on the paper.

Burn the paper and put the ashes in the center of the pentacle.

Then recite chant:

"Lord of Hell Bring Justice to the one who caused me misery - Satan I ask for your help."

Something very bad shall happen to that person in a week or less.

REVENGE SPELLS

Candle Revenge Spell

You Need:
13 black candles
A belonging of the intended victim
A cauldron
Black pepper

Cast a circle and and set up the 13 candles in a crown on your altar. Sprinkle the pepper around the circle while chanting:

"To lock in hate, to lock out love, rage I must create, Revenge I must think of."

Light the first candle and then say:
"I light thee with only hate in my heart. Only with revenge in mind. I give thee light to aid my rage into the direction of he/she I hate."

Light the other candles one by one and repeat this. Now hold the belonging tightly in both of your hands and visualize the persons face, and think of all the things he/she has done to you.

Gather all the hate and rage you have toward this person and force the energy into the object.

When you feel that you have succeeded in doing this, open your eyes and chant three times:

"Make (fill in name) see the hurt he/she brings me, make him/her feel the pain I feel.

Remove the hate from my heart, and all the pain he/she has brought me,

Move it towards the more deserving, all he/she has done he/she shall now see,

I will seek my revenge times three."

Now run the object through all 13 candles, and then drop it into the cauldron, and stare into the smoke as you chant:

"As this burns, your pain shall begin, and all you brought me, now shall end."

When the object has burnt out close the circle.

Picture Of Revenge

You Need:

Photo of the person
Matches

Begin by taking the photo of the desired Victim you wish to bind/curse and stare at it, long and hard. Let the hatred, pain and anger you hold escape into the Item.

Once you feel the emotions, tear the Item in half and place it on a stone surface outside and light it on fire with the match.

As the fire burns, repeat the following until the fire burns out:

*"As above and so below,
to the depths of hell,
your soul will go.
North, south, east, west,
revenge on you is what is best."*

When the fire is out, Take the ashes and scatter them and clean the area so no one knows what you were doing.

Tears Of Revenge

You Need:
1 black candle

Chant the following three times while sitting in front of a burning black candle;

"Every tear I cried May you suffer by and by.
Three times three make him/her see what he/she does to me
As I will it, So mote it be"

Revenge On An Ex Love

You Need:
1 picture of them
1 heart shaped locket
1 black candle
1 permanent marker Light the candle.

Write their first and last name on the back of the picture in the permanent marker.

Burn the picture in the candle. As the picture burns say the following:

"Your heart will burn forever, you'll see, you will never love anyone as much as you loved me."

Then put the ashes from the picture in the locket then bury it outside. Your ex will never find anyone as good as you as long as the locket is undisturbed. They will try to get back together with you, turn them down to really make this curse sting!

<u>Soul Killer Spell</u>

You Need:

3 black candles
1 picture of victim or enemy
matches/lighter

Place picture of your enemy in front of you on your alter.

Place one candle on the left of the picture, one on the right, and the final one to the top.

Now light the candles starting with the one above the picture, then the left, then the right.

Now chant the following 3 times:

"To the fires of hell your soul shall fly,

I send it screaming across the sky,

Where it shall endure eternal pain,

And slowly you shall go insane,

You will live as fate condemns,

Your soul destroyed until the end."

Snuff out the candles in reverse order.
(right, left, top)

Repeat this for 7 nights in a row.

<u>Nightmare Hex</u>

You Need:

1 black candle
Picture of the person you want to hex

Light the candle then while looking at the person and think of them having horrible nightmares, say:

"Phobetor, god of nightmares I call to you and ask you to bring nightmares to my enemy."

Then repeat this 3 times:

*"Dream of horror, dream of terror,
fear to sleep, tonight and forever."*

When you are done saying the incantation 3 times, burn the picture or rip it up then extinguish the candle.

The Black Dot

You Need:
Sheet of paper from the bible that contains Satan's name.
Black Paint.
1 One Candle Black.

First Take the sheet of Paper and write your enemies name onto it, After you have done so then paint a black dot onto a piece of paper and chant the following after lighting your candle.

*"_____ I call down the Wrath of hell upon you.
By this Blasphemy I curse you ___ In the name of the Evil.
I curse you In the name of all which is unholy.
I DAMN THEE FOR BETRAYING ME
I DAMN THEE FOR DISGRACING ME
I DAMN THEE FOR ALL THE PAIN THOU HATH CAUSED ME,
SO SHALL MY WILL BE DONE! AND SO MOTE IT BE!"*

Blow the candle out and pour a small drop onto the middle of the black dot.

Go find your target and either give this paper to them if they take it into there hand, then Wrath shall befall them!

They will continue to suffer until the paper is burned.

Red Revenge

You Need:

One Red Candle
New or waning moon
Picture of victim
Red pen or marker
Cauldron

Go to a secluded peaceful place (empty room,etc) at midnight on a new or waning moon. Light your candle and draw a red x on the victims face in the picture. Place the picture in your cauldron and use the candle to light the photo. After doing so chant:

*"This Person Has made me mad
I don't want them to be glad,
I take revenge on them tonight,
As I say these words with strife,
Make them pay, Make them pay,
So Mote It Be"*

By now the photo will be ashes. Take the ashes and keep them in a container. As long as you have the ashes the victim will suffer in pain. When you think they have had enough, throw away the ashes.

Graveyard Revenge

You Need:

Natural beeswax
Victim identity items (hair, nails, pieces of clothing, buttons)
Natural silk fabric
13 candles
Natural black thread
1 ritual shovel

This ritual is carried out only in 29 lunar day.

At 10 pm, at the altar light the all 13 black candles.

Fashion a doll out of the black fabric. Use the items that identify your victim to stuff the inside. Seal with beeswax.

After that wrap the doll with black thread 9 times, and say:

"___ (Name your enemy) From the light I see off to the side of darkness.
AN ALU BAR ANABA I point you the way to the churchyard, the coffin in the grave. "

After this, go to a graveyard. In the center of a grave (choose wisely!) dig a hole, to a depth of 1 foot.

Put the doll in the hole and cover it back up and say: "___ (name your enemy), you are going to lie. here is your new home."

Whatever killed the person who's grave you buried the doll in will befall your enemy.

Sore Revenge

You Need:

1 black candle
1 photo of target

Light the black candle and place a picture of your enemy in front of you.

Tilt the candle so the wax drips upon the would-be victim in the picture.

Visualize the wax burning sores into the body of your enemy.

While doing so, recite the following 3 times:

*"As the candle burns the sores will too,
vile lesions appear all over you."*

When finished, snuff the candle and leave the picture on your alter untouched for 3 nights.

CANDLE MAGICK

In candle magick the color of the candle must correspond with what the end goal of your spell is going to be.

It is also wise to anoint the candle with Dragons Blood oil first, then anoint the same candle with an oil that again, corresponds with your intended spell.

The colors are as follows:

Red: Courage and health, sexual love and lust

Pink: Friendship, sweet love

Orange: Attraction and encouragement

Gold: Financial gain, business endeavors

Yellow: Persuasion and protection

Green: Financial gain, abundance, fertility

Light Blue: Health, patience and understanding

Dark Blue: Depression and vulnerability

Purple: Ambition and power

Brown: Earth-related or animal-related workings

Black: Negativity and banishment

White: Purity and truth

Silver: Reflection, intuition, lunar connections

The spell work involved with candle magick is pretty straight forward. As stated in the previous section, the color matching your intent is the most important. The best part about candle magick is the ability to literally create your own spells.

But traditionally, this is how a candle spell would work:

Use a piece of colored paper that matches the color intent of your candle. Decide what your goal is, and write it on the piece of paper.

As you write down your goal, visualize yourself achieving that goal. Think about the different ways in which your goal might come true. Once you've written down your goal, fold the paper, concentrating on your intent the whole time.

Place one corner of the folded paper into the candle's flame and allow it to catch fire. Hold the paper as long as possible (without burning your fingers) and then place it in a fire-safe bowl or cauldron to burn completely.

Now allow the candle to burn out completely while meditating and concentrating on your end goal.

When the candle has burned out completely, dispose of it, typically by burying it.

DO NOT USE IT AGAIN!

Now keep in mind, the more elaborate your spell, such as incorporating herbs and incantations, the more powerful it will be.

Have Fun and be as creative as you can!!

<u>Summoning Spirits</u>

WARNING: The following spell work can be VERY DANGEROUS! DO NOT Attempt these spells unless you really know what you are doing and even then – do so AT YOUR OWN RISK!

The following spell work is to summon a handful of helpful spirits. The ritual is the same for all of them, all you have to do is swap out the name and symbol for the spirit you wish to call, depending on your goal. It is important to remember that you must banish the spirit when done, otherwise they will not leave on their own.

The Summoning Ritual:

At midnight with a full moon bright in the sky;

Create a huge pentagram on the ground.

The 5th point must face south.

Place a large black candle at each point.

Light the south facing one first and then light the rest counter clockwise with you standing within the center of the pentagram.

Sit down and face south.

Chant the following 3 times:
*"Here this star I consecrate,
part the clouds and open the gates."*

Now, have the name of the spirit you are about to conjure written on a piece of parchment paper.

Place it in front of you. Hold a black ink pen on your hand and place it on the paper under where you have the spirits name written.

Close your eyes, and breath deep.

Call the spirits name over and over. Say the name, take a slow deep breath, say the name again. Do this at least 7 times.

Try not to be distracted by any noises your hear around you. When you begin to feel a presence around you ask the spirit to take your hand and write his name.

Do not resist, let your hand scribble out whatever you conjured up. It will not be in any language you recognize, it will most likely be a weird symbol of some sort.

Once this happens, proceed to greet him/her and ask of him/her whatever task you conjured them for.

When you are done giving him his task, you must tell him to leave!

Simply break your concentration, open your eyes and chant the following 3 times:

*"Do as I command, the task at hand,
return to your lair, be gone as I stand!"*

Now stand up and proceed to snuff out the candles in the reverse order you lit them.

Now take the paper with the names on it and fold it 4 times. Keep it hidden somewhere safe.

If the paper is destroyed, the task will be canceled.

Spirits You Can Summon With This Spell:

Temirgoth – Keeper of hidden knowledge. Often appears as a black crow.

Baxtversa – Stealer of hearts, cupid from Hell. Often appears as handsome man.

Vacagor – Demon Assassin. Use With Caution. Often appears in reptilian form.

Geshwer – Offers protection. Often appears as horse with lions head.

Zokodac – Keeper of great wealth. Often appears as kindly old man.

Braadvegth – Starts wars. Often appears as a large black vulture.

Xzgaath – Brings lust and desire. Often appears as beautiful woman.

*While all may not take on a physical form due to the energy it consumes, if they do, they are most likely to appear in the forms given, but not always.

MAGICKAL ITEMS, OILS & HERBS

MAGICKAL ITEMS

Altar
A special surface set aside exclusively for magical workings or religious acknowledgment.

Amulet
A magically charged object which deflects specific, usually negative energies. Generally, a protective object.

Athame
A black(typically) handled, double sided blade, ritual knife. Its purpose is strictly symbolic. The athame is used to direct Personal Power during ritual workings. It represents the male aspect of divinity and can be used to cast and cut a circle during ritual as well as to direct energy in much the same way as a wand.

Book of Shadows
A hand written journal you keep of all of the spells and rituals you have performed. Record what you did and when as well as the results.

Cauldron
The cauldron is a symbol of rebirth, the hearth, of abundance and of well being. Cauldrons represent the female aspect of divinity and the womb.

Grimoire
A spell book or magical workbook containing ritual information, formulae, magical properties of objects and preparation of ritual equipment.

Magick Circle
A sphere constructed of Personal Power in which rituals are usually enacted. The term refers to the circle that marks the sphere's penetration of the ground, for it extends both above and below it.

Pentacle
A ritual object (usually a circular piece of wood,metal,clay etc) upon which a five-pointed star (pentagram) is inscribed, painted or engraved. It represents the element of Earth. A pentacle is a pentagram with a circle surrounding it.

Sigil
A magically oriented seal, sign, glyph, or other device used in magical working.

Talisman
An object ritually charged with power to attract a specific force or energy to its bearer.

Wand
A wand, or a rod, is a stick that has been carefully gathered and prepared to be used for ritual work. They are associated with masculine energy and the element of air or fire depending on the tradition. Wands are used for pointing and focusing energy, and for stirring.

MAGICKAL OILS

AMBER
Use to enhance and inspire love, comfort and happiness, help in ritual and spell work, to attract these things.

AMBERGRIS
Enhance and direct psychic ability, in rituals and spells rooted in psychic ventures, helping to bring the subconscious to the attention of the conscious.

BAYBERRY
Potent aid involving protection and control. Keep negative energies at bay or more completely harness the energies you wish to direct.

BAY LAUREL
Healing, Protection, Psychic, Purification, Strength

BLACK OPIUM
Draws one into the realm of the mysterious and the hidden, open awareness, to deepen ability , open hidden worlds and seek out mysteries.

CARDAMON
Aphrodisiac, Love

CORIANDER
Healing, Love

CYPRESS
Comfort, Healing, Protection

DRAGONS BLOOD
Adds great strength and power to magick and spells.

EGYPTIAN MUSK
Potent aid in spells and rituals, divination, enhance and increase the wisdom gained through such magic, blessings and rituals seeking an increased strength in magic, willpower, or spirit.

EUCALYPTUS
Healing, Visions

JASMINE
Dreams, Love, Money

LAVENDER
Happiness, Love, Peace, Protection, Purification

MARJORAM
Happiness, Health, Love, Money, Protection

PALMAROSA
Healing, Love

ROSEMARY
Healing, Love, Protection, Purification

ROSE OTTO
Healing, Love, Protection

SANDALWOOD
Healing, Protection, Spirituality

WHITE THYME
Healing, Purification

MAGICKAL HERBS

ALOE
Beauty, protection, success, peace

ANGELICA
Protection, Exorcism

ANISE
Protection, purification, awareness, joy

BASIL
Protection, love, wealth, healing relationships, ensuring faithfulness in a mate, courage, fertility, exorcism

BAY LEAVES
Psychic visions and dreams, repels negativity and evil

CINNAMON
Spiritual quests, augmenting power, love, success, psychic work, healing, cleansing

CLOVE
Money matters, visions, cleansing and purification

CORIANDER
Protection of home and serenity, peace, longevity and love spells

DANDELION
Divination, enhance psychic dreams and second sight

DRAGONS BLOOD
Love, protection, exorcism, sexual potency, magical power,

energy, strength, purification, cleansing

FENNEL
Purification, protection, healing, money

FRANKINCENSE
Powerful aid to meditation, purify ritual spaces and invoke a spiritual frame of mind.

GARLIC
Protective herb, healing, courage, exorcism

GINGER
Power, success, love, money matters

GINSENG
Love, wishes, beauty, desire

HAWTHORN
Promotes happiness in marriage or a relationship

HENBANE
Attract the love of a woman. Once used as an ingredient in a Witches flying ointment

HIGH JOHN
Increase charm strength, drawing luck, gaining mastery, and strengthening the libido of men.

HYSSOP
Purification baths, protective and banishing spells

IRON WEED
Carry in a purple flannel bag for control over others

JASMINE
Love spells, charms and sachets

JUNIPER
Protection against accidents, harm and theft

KAVA KAVA
Aphrodisiac, potions, induces visions, astral work, travel protection, success and job promotion

KOLA NUT
Peace, removing depression, and calming

LAVENDER
Love, protection, healing, sleep, purification, and peace. Promotes healing

LEMON GRASS
Psychic cleansing and opening, lust potions

LICORICE
Love, lust, and fidelity. Carry to attract a lover

LILAC
Wisdom, memory, good luck and spiritual aid

MANDRAKE
Protection, prosperity, fertility, and exorcising evil

MARJORAM
Cleansing, purification, and dispelling negativity

MILK THISTLE
Strength, perseverance, wisdom, aid in decision making

MORNING GLORY
Binding, banishing, and promoting attraction

MOTHERWORT
Bolstering ego, building confidence, success and counter magick

MUGWORT
Increase lust and fertility, prevent backache, cure disease and madness

MYRRH
Spiritual opening, meditation, and healing. This herb has high psychic vibrations that will enhance any magickal working.

NETTLE
Dispelling darkness and fear, strengthening the will

NUTMEG
Attracting money/prosperity, bringing luck, protection, and breaking hexes.

OLIVE LEAF
Peace, potency, fertility, healing, protection and lust

OSHA ROOT
Protection against evil spirits

PASSION FLOWER
Attracting friendship and prosperity and heightening libido

PATCHOULI
Spells, sachets, baths and mixtures for money and love

PENNYROYAL
Peace and tranquility

ROSE HIPS
Healing spells and mixtures, brings good luck, calls in good spirits

RUE
Healing, health, mental powers, freedom and protection against the evil eye

SAGE
Self purification, improve mental ability and bring wisdom. Promotes spiritual, mental, emotional and physical health and longevity.

SANDALWOOD
Scatter sandalwood powder around the home to clear it of negativity. Burn during protection, healing, and exorcism spells.

SARSAPARILLA
Sexual vitality, health, love and money. Mix with sandalwood and cinnamon and sprinkle around home or business to draw money.

SCULLCAP
Bind oaths and consecrate vows and commitments.

ST. JOHN'S WORT
Protects against all forms of black witchcraft, protection and blessing, banish spirits and demons.

STAR ANISE
Increase psychic awareness & abilities

THISTLE
Healing, protection

TOBACCO
Promotes peace, confidence, and personal strength. Also used for banishing. Mix with salt and burn with a black candle to win a court case.

UVA URSI
Increasing intuitive and psychic powers

VALERIAN
Dream magick, reconciliation, love, and harmony

VENUS FLYTRAP
Love and protection

VERVAIN
Protection, purification, money, youth, peace, healing, and sleep

WHITE SAGE
Use as an incense, for smudging or for purification.

WORMWOOD
Remove anger, stop war, inhibit violent acts, and for protection from the evil eye.

YARROW
Healing, divination, draws love, banish negativity, ward off fear, and promote courage, confidence, and psychic opening.

YELLOW DOCK
Fertility, healing and money. Sprinkle an infusion of yellow dock around a place of business to attract customers.

YERBA MATE
Fidelity, love and lust. Worn to attract the opposite sex

YEW
Raising the dead, protection against evil, immortality, and breaking hexes.

YLANG YLANG
Increases sexual attraction and persuasiveness. Promotes calm, peaceful relaxation and relieves anxiety and depression.

YOHIMBE BARK
Love, lust, virility and fertility, curing impotency, cursing

NOTES: